Konichiwa,
JAPAN

by Leah Kaminski

CHERRY LAKE PUBLISHING • ANN ARBOR, MICHIGAN

Published in the United States of America by Cherry Lake Publishing
Ann Arbor, Michigan
www.cherrylakepublishing.com

Reading Adviser: Marla Conn MS, Ed., Literacy specialist, Read-Ability, Inc.

Book Design: Book Buddy Media

Photo Credits: ©yorkfoto/Getty Images, cover (top); ©Pamela Lao/Getty Images, cover (bottom); ©Pexels/Pixabay, 1; ©ayzek/Getty Images, 3; ©xegxef/Pixabay, 4; ©Sharleen Chao/Getty Images, 5; ©BardoczPeter/Getty Images, 6; ©Martin Pflaume/EyeEm/Getty Images, 7; ©tawatchaiprakobkit/Getty Images, 8; ©Eloise Campbell/Getty Images, 9; ©Koichi Kamoshida/Getty Images, 10; ©Koichi Kamoshida/Getty Images, 11; ©Nicman/Pixabay, 12 (top); ©andrew_t8/Pixabay, 12 (bottom); ©Unknown/Wikimedia, 13; ©Indeed/Getty Images, 14; ©Mark Runnacles/Getty Images, 15; ©mrtom-uk/Getty Images, 16 (top); ©LaChouettePhoto/Getty Images, 16 (bottom); ©ebenart/Getty Images, 17; ©Koichi Kamoshida/Getty Images, 18; ©US Library of Congress/Wikimedia, 19; ©US Government/Wikimedia, 20; ©NicolasMcComber/Getty Images, 22; ©Niabot/Wikimedia, 23 (top); ©DigiPub/Getty Images, 23 (middle); ©Toyohara Chikanobu/Wikimedia, 23 (bottom); ©xavierarnau/Getty Images, 24; ©pullia/Getty Images, 25; ©eAlisa/Getty Images, 26; ©Fumiaki Shingu/Wikimedia, 27; ©Pixelchrome Inc/Getty Images, 28; ©Chris McGrath/Getty Images, 29; ©Junko Kimura/Getty Images, 30; ©Carl Court/Getty Images, 31; ©ahsandford/Pixabay, 32; ©1278956/Pixabay, 33; ©Junko Kimura/Getty Images, 34; ©magicflute002/Getty Images, 35; ©kei_gokei/Getty Images, 36; ©Emil Lyu/EyeEm/Getty Images, 37; ©Photographer is my life./Getty Images, 38; ©artparadigm/Getty Images, 39; ©tbralnina/Getty Images, 40; ©jatuporn amorntangsati/Getty Images, 41; ©Rimma_Bondarenko/Getty Images, 42; ©xamtiw/Getty Images, 43; ©The Picture Pantry/Getty Images, 44; ©MAHATHIR MOHD YASIN/Shutterstock, 45; ©filo/Getty Images, background

Copyright ©2020 by Cherry Lake Publishing
All rights reserved. No part of this book may be reproduced or utilized in any form
or by any means without written permission from the publisher.

Library of Congress Cataloging-in-Publication Data has been filed and is available at catalog.loc.gov

Cherry Lake Publishing would like to acknowledge the work of The Partnership for 21st Century Learning.
Please visit www.p21.org for more information.

Printed in the United States of America
Corporate Graphics

TABLE OF CONTENTS

CHAPTER 1

WELCOME TO JAPAN!

Japan is called Nippon or Nihon by its citizens. The name "Japan" came from Italian explorer Marco Polo. He based it on how the Chinese said the word Nippon. There has been a long relationship between Japan and foreign nations. This relationship is an important part of Japanese history and culture. The balance between old and new traditions is also crucial to understanding Japan.

The city of Tokyo has a population of more than 13 million people.

Japan is an island country with a very beautiful environment. Nature is valuable to Japan's people. They can enjoy everything from mountains to beaches. Their forests are full of evergreens, maple trees that turn red in the fall, and cherry trees with pink blossoms. The cherry tree is Japan's national tree.

In Japan, most cherry trees are grown for their flowers and not their fruit.

ACTIVITY

Place a piece of paper over the map of Japan and trace the country's borders. Japan's four major islands are Honshu, Hokkaido, Kyushu, and Shikoku. There are also many smaller islands. One group of these islands is often referred to as the Ryukyu Islands. Use an atlas to find this group of small islands. Label them on your map. Use a star to represent Tokyo, Japan's capital.

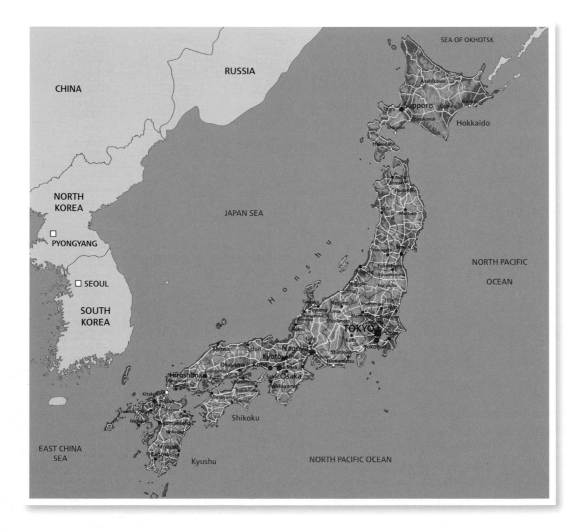

Tokyo spreads across 850 square miles (2,201 square kilometers), about the size of Chicago, Illinois.

Japan is an archipelago, or chain of islands, off the east coast of Asia. The islands stretch through the ocean for 1,500 miles (2,400 km). There are four major islands. The largest island is Honshu. Japan's largest cities are on Honshu, including Tokyo. Tokyo is the nation's capital city. Other major cities on Honshu are Hiroshima, Kobe, Kyoto, and Osaka. There are also 6,848 smaller islands in Japan!

Mount Fuji last erupted in 1707. Scientists think it might erupt again in the future.

To the east of Japan's archipelago is the Pacific Ocean. To the west is the Sea of Japan. Across the Sea of Japan lie South Korea, North Korea, and Russia.

Volcanic eruptions formed the landscape. Rugged volcanic mountains cover four-fifths of the country. This includes the famous Mount Fuji, Japan's tallest peak.

Violent volcanic eruptions still occur frequently. Japan has more than 100 active volcanoes. The country experiences thousands of earthquake tremors yearly. There were two deadly earthquakes in 2018, one in Osaka and one in Hokkaido. These earthquakes sometimes trigger tsunamis. Japan has warning systems that help people survive these disasters.

A Major National Tragedy

In 2011, a tsunami following an earthquake caused the Fukushima Daiichi nuclear disaster. The tsunami disabled important equipment at a nuclear power plant. As a result, there were meltdowns and explosions. It was the second-worst nuclear accident in history. Radioactive material was released into the soil and into the Pacific Ocean, even reaching the Western United States.

Some populations of cranes come to Japan to spend the winter there.

Japan's climate is varied. The north has four seasons, including a very snowy winter. The south is tropical. Japan's island climate also creates a summer rainy season. It is called the *bai-u* ("plum rain") because it begins when the plums ripen. Late summer is the high season for typhoons. Typhoons are hurricanes that form in the western Pacific Ocean.

Humans have changed the Japanese environment. For example, acid rain is created by power plant emissions. It damages the water supply for aquatic life. The air and water are also polluted by factories and poor waste management. Land use for housing and agriculture has taken **habitat** from native plants and animals. **Deforestation** is also a major problem.

A History of Japanese Whaling

The Japanese began hunting for whales in the 12th century. Whaling continues today with large-scale whaling for profit. Whaling is controversial. Japan wants to protect this cultural practice. Outside groups believe the protection of the animals is more important than tradition. In late 2018, Japan defied international rules against whaling and plans to continue hunting whales.

All of these issues threaten the well-being of Japan's wildlife. Once-common animals are extinct. Others, like the crested ibis, were once considered extinct in the wild but with hard work are being reintroduced. Much more work must be done to save these **endangered** plants and animals.

Kingfishers can be seen perched on branches or flying low over many of Japan's waterways.

Japan is a major route for migrating birds. The country has many water birds and also a rich variety of sea life. Japan's land and water are very **ecologically** diverse. About one-quarter of the country's vertebrate species are endemic. Endemic means they only exist in one place. Thirty-one Japanese animals are designated as critically endangered.

Snow Monkey

The Japanese macaque, or snow monkey, has adjusted well to Japan 's cold winters. When macaques need to warm up, they take dips in hot springs. The population of these clever monkeys is declining. They are losing habitat. They are also killed when they raid local farms for food.

CHAPTER 2

BUSINESS AND GOVERNMENT IN JAPAN

From 660 BCE until after World War II (1939–1945), emperors ruled Japan. In 1946, a new constitution made the emperor the symbolic head of the country. Now, Japan is a constitutional **monarchy**. This means power rests with the people.

The Emperor of Japan lives in the Imperial Palace. Visitors can join a guided tour of the grounds, but are not allowed inside the buildings.

ACTIVITY

"Kimigayo" is the Japanese national anthem. It promotes peace and success. The song traces its origin to a *waka*, a traditional song-poem written in the 10th century. See below for the lyrics and their translation. Then learn how to sing "Kimigayo." With an adult, look online for sound clips of the anthem for help with the tune and pronunciation.

JAPANESE LYRICS:

Kimigayo wa

chiyo ni yachiyo ni

sazareishi no

iwao to narite

koke no musu made

ENGLISH TRANSLATION:

May your reign

Continue for a thousand, eight thousand generations,

Until the pebbles

Grow into boulders

Lush with moss

Students might sing "Kimigayo" at special events, such as sports games and graduation ceremonies.

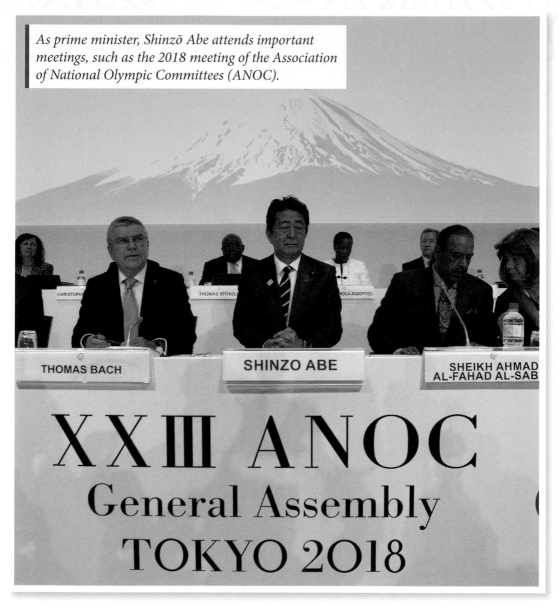

As prime minister, Shinzō Abe attends important meetings, such as the 2018 meeting of the Association of National Olympic Committees (ANOC).

THOMAS BACH

SHINZO ABE

SHEIKH AHMAD AL-FAHAD AL-SAB

XXIII ANOC
General Assembly
TOKYO 2018

The Japanese prime minister is the head of three branches of government. This is similar to the United States. The current prime minister is Shinzō Abe. The Diet is the legislature. It has two houses. The House of Councillors (*Sangi-in*) has 241 members. The House of Representatives (*Shugi-in*) has 465 seats.

Prefectures are the Japanese version of states. Local assemblies are elected directly. They hold much of the power over day-to-day life. Education, pollution control, and other things are dealt with by the local assemblies. All citizens 18 years or older can vote in local and national elections.

An Important Crop

Rice grows well in Japan because of its rain. For 2,000 years, Japanese mountainsides have been covered with rice terraces where water drains from paddy to paddy. The written character for "rice field" is part of many last names. Rice paddies are man-made wetlands, beautiful and ecologically rich.

In Japan, it is not unusual to see a European-style church with a Japanese-style garden.

Japan has a long history of taking foreign traditions and making them its own. Today, Japan is influenced by Asia, Europe, and the United States. But Japan has interacted with foreign countries for centuries. Hundreds of years ago, the Japanese adopted many customs from China. Some examples are the way they grew rice, their writing system, and the religion of Buddhism. All of these became significant to Japan's culture. In the 1500s, Portugal discovered Japan, and the island country began to trade with European nations. European cultural influences, such as Catholicism, came to Japan.

Between 2.6 and 3.1 million Japanese lives were lost in World War II. People today honor their sacrifice with special events.

After seeing Europe invading other Asian nations, Japanese leaders decided that foreign influence was not a good idea. They closed the country off for about 200 years. In the 1800s, Japanese leaders wanted to compete with the West. Japan embraced a Western style of government and grew its military. Japan's desire to expand was part of what led it to fight against the United States in WWII.

Japanese Robots

Japan has been the source of many technological inventions, such as camera phones. Encouraged by Prime Minister Abe, Japanese scientists are now making exciting progress with robots. New products in 2018 include a lovable pet robot and robot waiters that can be controlled by people with disabilities.

The attack on Pearl Harbor lasted less than two hours. More than 50 Japanese and 2,400 Americans were killed.

In 1941, the United States prevented Japan from receiving needed oil. This is called an embargo. The embargo helped China in Japan's war against that country. In response, Japan attacked U.S. Navy ships at Pearl Harbor in Hawaii. The U.S. then entered WWII on the side of Britain and a group of nations called the Allies. Japan was on the side of the Axis nations, including Germany and Italy.

After the war, Japan's economy was ruined. Japan was occupied by the Allies and continued to follow Western economic practices. Eventually, Japan's economy became one of the biggest in the world.

Japan is one of the world's largest manufacturers of automobiles and consumer electronics. However, services employ the most people. Services are actions people perform. Services include advertising, tourism, and healthcare. In 2017, 25.58 percent of Japanese workers were employed in industry and 70.93 percent in services.

A Tragic History

In August 1945, American planes dropped atomic bombs on the cities of Hiroshima and Nagasaki. 66,000 people died immediately in Hiroshima, 39,000 in Nagasaki, and many more thousands later died from radiation. Japan surrendered days after the bombings, ending WWII. These bombs remain the only nuclear weapons ever used in war.

Japan is the world's fourth-largest exporter. China and the United States are its largest export partners. These and other countries buy Japan's steel goods, automobiles, and technology.

Japan lacks **natural resources.** It must import fossil fuels, coal, and most minerals. Because it is so mountainous, it does not have much farming land. This means just over half of Japan's food must be imported. Rice farming is the only major form of agriculture.

JAPAN'S IMPORTS AND EXPORTS

Do you want to know more about Japan's economy? Take a look at its trading partners. Trading partners are the countries that import goods from a country or export goods to that country. Here is a graph showing the countries that are Japan's top import and export trading partners.

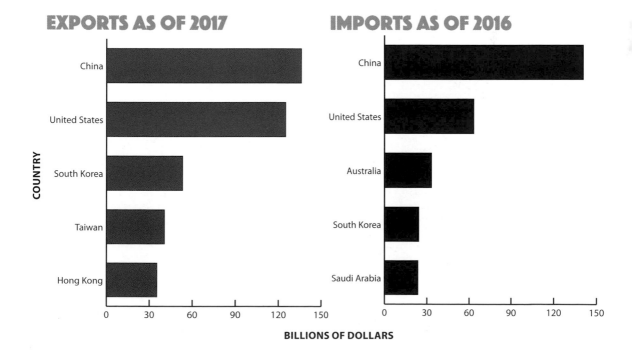

EXPORTS AS OF 2017

IMPORTS AS OF 2016

BILLIONS OF DOLLARS

CHAPTER 3

MEET THE PEOPLE

A balanced diet, high quality medical services, and an active lifestyle contribute to a healthy older population in Japan.

As of 2018, Japan's population was 126 million. It is the 11th-most populous country. Two-thirds of Japanese people live in **urban** areas. Nearly one-quarter of the country's population lives in and around Tokyo!

Japan has laws that create a very low number of immigrants. Japan's population is about 98 percent Japanese. Because of low immigration, a low birth rate, and high life expectancy, Japan has the highest percentage of elderly citizens in the world. As of 2018, one out of five Japanese people is over the age of 70.

Japanese is the official language of Japan. The written language uses characters that represent words or combinations of words. One set of characters is called *kanji*.

ふたなり

Hiragana

Katakana and kanji

Turban Shell

Kanji

Kanji *is one of three writing systems used in Japan. People often use a combination of two or three writing systems.*

Most Japanese students start to study science in the third grade.

Education is highly valued in Japan. School is difficult and competitive. About half of all high school students attend a "cram school" called a *juku* to help them prepare for college entrance exams. Adult education is very popular too. Japanese people learn throughout their lives. Ninety-nine percent of Japanese people are literate, which means they can read and write. To compare, 86 percent of Americans can read and write.

Traditional Japanese art is known for balancing simplicity and detail. Calligraphy (beautiful handwriting), origami (folding paper into shapes), and *ikebana* (flower-arranging) are esteemed traditional art forms. Each of these art forms turn simple, daily things into art. Short haiku poems are another example of the Japanese love for simplicity and nature. Western art is very well liked, especially classical music. Tokyo alone has eight orchestras, and Japanese classical musicians are some of the best in the world.

Ikebana *was originally a way to make beautiful religious offerings.*

A variety of shapes and many different types of animals can be made through origami.

ACTIVITY

Origami is the art of paper folding. Try making an origami dog's head.

MATERIALS

- 1 square of brown construction paper, 8 inches (20 centimeters) by 8 inches (20 cm)
- black marker

INSTRUCTIONS

1. Working on a flat surface, fold the square of paper diagonally to form a triangle.

2. Pretend the triangle is an arrowhead. The arrow should be pointing towards you. Fold the left-hand and right-hand points of the triangle down. This forms the dog's ears.

3. Fold the point that is closest to you (the one forming a pointy "chin") back. This creates a flat chin for the dog.

4. Depending on the angles of the folds you created in step 3, there may or may not be a point at the top of the dog's head. If there is, fold this top point away from you. This creates a flat head for the dog.

5. Using a marker, draw eyes and a nose on the dog's face.

6. Try making several versions with different sizes and colors of paper.

Japanese culture today is an exciting mix of new and old, foreign and local. Young Japanese people are known for fast trends and daring street fashion. They make Western styles their own. One popular fashion is "fairy *kei*," where pastel outfits are inspired by children's toys like Care Bears. Another is the **Victorian**-inspired "Lolita" style, often mixed with punk fashions.

The kimono is a traditional gown with a V-neck and long sleeves, secured with a wide sash across the waist.

Western-style pop music is very well liked in Japan. "J-pop" is one style influenced by the West that also has roots in traditional Japanese music. Japanese sports are also influenced by the West. While sumo wrestling is over 1,000 years old, the newer sport of baseball is the most-watched sport in the country.

In sumo wrestling, opponents try to push each other out of a ring that is 15 feet (4.55 meters) across.

A Japanese Baseball Tradition

Americans introduced baseball to Japan in the 19th century. There is a large professional league, but national high school tournaments are even more popular. Several very famous Major League Baseball (MLB) players have been from Japan. Some are Ichiro Suzuki and Hideo Nomo, and current star for the LA Angels Shohei Ohtani .

CHAPTER 4

CELEBRATIONS

Family life in Japan revolves around work and school. However, there are many fun holidays that the whole country celebrates. New Year's is Japan's most important holiday. It lasts a few days. Starting at midnight on December 31, people visit shrines and temples. The Bon Festival in late summer is also very famous. It is a 500-year-old Buddhist holiday that honors the spirits of ancestors. To celebrate, people attend public festivals and visit graves.

Japanese people hold special festivals called matsuri. *Each matsuri is based on a specific Shinto temple.*

Golden Week is several holidays grouped in a single week. It begins with Shōwa Day, which honors the previous emperor. It also includes Constitution Memorial Day, Greenery Day, and Children's Day.

On Children's Day, parents fly kites in their children's honor. There are other holidays especially for children. For example, *Shichi-Go-San*, or 7-5-3 Day, celebrates the ages of 3, 5, and 7. These ages are milestones in a Japanese child's life. Parents take their children to Shinto shrines to pray for their well-being.

Festival participants often wear historical garments and makeup.

Japan is a very urban nation, but it has kept its natural roots. Seasonal rhythms are a meaningful part of celebrations in Japan. Respect for nature is central to Japan's ancient Shinto religion. For example, Mount Fuji is an ancient **pilgrimage** site. It is one of the religion's Three Holy Mountains.

CHART OF HOLIDAYS

These are some holidays that are celebrated in Japan:

Second Monday of January **Coming of Age Day**

February 3 or 4 *Setsubun*

February 11 **National Foundation Day**

March 3 **Girls' Day or Doll Festival**

March 20 or 21 **Spring Equinox**

April 29 *Shōwa* **Day**

May 3 **Constitution Memorial Day**

May 4 **Greenery Day**

May 5 **Children's Day**

Third Monday of July **Marine Day**

August 11 **Mountain Day**

Third Monday of September **Respect for the Aged Day**

September 23 or 24 **Autumn Equinox**

November 3 **Culture Day**

November 15 *Shichi-Go-San*

November 23 **Labor Thanksgiving Day**

December 23 **Emperor's birthday**

ACTIVITY

Japanese families fly kites shaped like carp, a type of fish, as part of Children's Day celebrations. How about making your own?

MATERIALS

- large sheets of white paper
- tape
- crayons
- craft wire
- wire cutters
- 2 feet (0.6 m) of string
- a ruler
- scissors

INSTRUCTIONS

1. Draw a fish shape on a piece of white paper. The fish should be 12 inches (30 cm) long, 4 inches (10 cm) wide at the body, and 6 inches (15 cm) wide at the tail. The mouth should be 2 inches (5 cm) wide. Use a ruler to measure these dimensions. Draw a separate fin. Cut out the fin and fish shapes.

2. Trace your cut-out fish and fin shapes on another section of white paper, and cut out the new shapes to create the other side of the fish and a second fin.

3. Tape both sides of the fish together along the edges. Leave the mouth and the end of the tail open. Tape one fin onto each side of the fish.

4. Color your fish kite with crayons.

5. Use scissors to make cuts around the fish's mouth. The cuts should be 0.25 inches (0.6 cm) long and spaced 0.25 inches (0.6 cm) apart.

6. Use craft wire and wire cutters to carefully form a circle that is 1.25 inches (3.2 cm) in diameter.

7. Place this wire ring just inside the fish's mouth. Bend the paper tabs over the wire ring. Tape the tabs in place. This should keep the fish's mouth open.

8. Tape the ends of the string to each side of the fish's mouth. Grab the string and have fun making the fish swim and dance through the air.

During carp streamer festivals, parents hang kites to bring good health and success to their sons.

Many Japanese families take trips to temples to admire nature and reflect on their spirituality.

Many holidays reflect nature's importance to Japanese people. The fall and spring **equinoxes** are holidays related to Shintoism and Buddhism. *Sakura zensen* is "the cherry blossom front." During this time, cherry trees blossom, starting in the south of Japan and continuing north. Groups of people gather for *hanami*, or "flower viewing," and spend time outdoors to admire the light-pink blossoms. In the fall, maple leaves turn color in a southward direction. The search for these beautiful red maple leaves is called *momijigari*. There are also national holidays called Marine Day and Mountain Day. Both holidays were created to honor the natural elements.

The Japanese zodiac calendar is made up of a 12-year cycle. Each year in the calendar cycle is represented by a different animal. Children born under an animal's sign are believed to take on certain characteristics. A child born in the year of the rat, for example, should be clever, creative, and hard working.

ZODIAC

2010 Year of the Tiger

2011 Year of the Rabbit

2012 Year of the Dragon

2013 Year of the Snake

2014 Year of the Horse

2015 Year of the Sheep

2016 Year of the Monkey

2017 Year of the Rooster

2018 Year of the Dog

2019 Year of the Boar

2020 Year of the Rat

2021 Year of the Ox

2022 Year of the Tiger

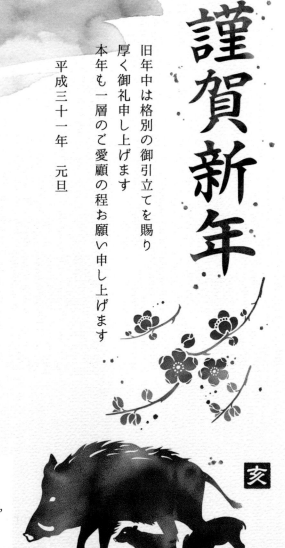

謹賀新年

平成三十一年　元旦

旧年中は格別の御引立てを賜り
厚く御礼申し上げます
本年も一層のご愛顧の程お願い申し上げます

亥

People born during the Year of the Boar are said to be kind and responsible, but sometimes lazy.

Temples and statues of the Buddha can be found across Japan.

Many of the Japanese holidays involve prayer, visits to shrines, or honoring one's ancestors. About 80 percent of Japanese people follow Shintoism. Sixty-six percent follow Buddhism. These numbers add up to more than 100 percent because many people belong to both religions. Shinto means "the way of the gods." Shintoism blends ancient Japanese traditions with respect for nature, ancestors, and spirits. Buddhists follow the teachings of Siddhartha Gautama, called the Buddha. Buddhism encourages followers to remember the fleeting nature of life, to be aware of their thoughts and actions, and to seek wisdom. Buddhist values inform much of Japanese culture, from their graceful art to their honor for the elderly.

CHAPTER 5

WHAT'S FOR DINNER?

The center of an everyday Japanese meal is a bowl of rice. It is eaten at nearly every meal. Sticky rice is part of desserts, and rice is even made into wine and vinegar! Fish dishes like sushi and sashimi are also key parts of the Japanese diet. Tofu is used in traditional Buddhist cooking, which is vegetarian. Ramen, a kind of noodle soup, was only imported to Japan a century ago but is now very common.

Following a Buddhist tradition, Japanese cooks try to use five colors in their dishes—white, black, red, green, and yellow.

A traditional Japanese meal seeks balance between different textures and flavors.

A traditional Japanese breakfast includes rice, miso soup, and side dishes. Typical side dishes include grilled fish, pickles, or dried seaweed (*nori*). Rice or noodles in soup is a common lunchtime meal. People often bring a lunch box (*bento*) to school or work. Rice balls (*onogiri*), sushi rolls, and steamed rice are frequently packed for lunch. Dinner is the main meal of the day.

There are about
20 different types
of Japanese ramen.

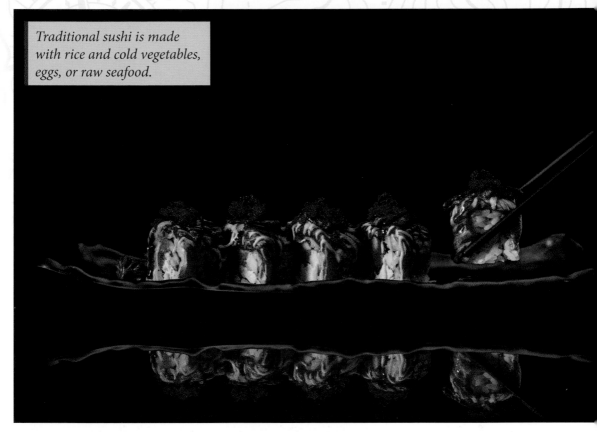

Traditional sushi is made with rice and cold vegetables, eggs, or raw seafood.

Japanese **cuisine** is known for delicate tastes and textures. Much of Japanese food is raw or only lightly cooked. Cooks pay attention to the visual presentation of the food. Diners use chopsticks, a Chinese invention adopted by the Japanese. Chopsticks are called *hashi*.

There are many special Japanese ways of preparing food. Tempura is when vegetables and meats are battered and fried. Cooking on a grill is also popular. *Hibachi* grilling requires cooking over hot coals. *Teppanyaki* cooking involves grilling meat or fish on a very hot iron plate. Meat, fish, and vegetables are stir-fried and seasoned with soy sauce or teriyaki sauce. Grilled and stir-fried foods are served with rice or noodles.

Black sesame seeds are a common garnish, adding a pleasant taste and look to a dish.

Vegetables often found in Japanese cuisine are mung bean sprouts, cabbage, daikon, turnips, and taro root. For seasoning, cooks use soy sauce, ginger, seaweed, fish flakes, wasabi, and miso. Wasabi is spicy horseradish, and miso is soybean paste.

RECIPE

Try this recipe for teriyaki vegetables. This dish requires chopping vegetables and working with hot oil over a stovetop. Be sure to ask an adult for help.

INGREDIENTS:

- 1 small onion, peeled
- 1 zucchini
- 1 carrot
- salt and pepper
- 2 tablespoons (30 milliliters) of cooking oil
- 1/4 cup (60 ml) of teriyaki sauce

INSTRUCTIONS

1. Rinse the zucchini and carrot. Clean the carrot with a vegetable peeler.

2. Have an adult slice the onion into very thin pieces. Next, he or she should slice the zucchini on an angle into thin pieces. The carrot should be sliced thinly too.

3. Have an adult heat the skillet over medium-high heat and carefully add the oil.

4. When the oil is hot, stir-fry the vegetables until the onions and zucchini are golden brown. Use tongs to stir everything.

5. Sprinkle lightly with salt and pepper.

6. Add the teriyaki sauce and stir well.

7. A great way to serve these vegetables is over rice. Give it a try!

Noodles, Broth, and Grilled Meats

There are thousands of ramen shops in Japan. There are even chains of ramen shops. Many varieties of ramen exist. They are all based on broth, wheat noodles, and toppings like grilled meats, eggs, and vegetables. Like so many other Japanese things, ramen originated in China, and Japan made it special.

Japanese cities have many restaurants. Japanese people love eating out. All types of food from around the world are popular in Japanese restaurants. If you want to find Japanese food, ramen shops and sushi restaurants are easy to find. You can also find *okonomiyaki* restaurants, where the savory pancakes called *okonomiyaki* are prepared in front of you. Or sometimes diners even prepare *okonomiyaki* on their own! Restaurants are just like the rest of Japan. They take the best of what's foreign and local, what's new and old, and they make it their own. What part of Japan will you explore next?

Current Natural Disasters

Japanese people chose the *kanji* character *sai* (災), meaning "disaster," to be the country's symbol for 2018. International news about Japan that year focused on the many natural disasters its people endured. Just from July to September there was a major flood and a heatwave with the highest temperatures on record. There was also the strongest typhoon to hit in 25 years, and a 6.7 magnitude earthquake in Hokkaido. All of these resulted in deaths. Some of the weather-related disasters can be tied to climate change. These disasters were even bad enough to shrink the country's economy.

GLOSSARY

cuisine *(kwi-ZEEN)* a style or way of cooking or presenting food

deforestation *(dee-for-iss-TAY-shun)* the removal of trees and forests for human use

ecologically *(ee-kuh-LAH-jik-uh-lee)* having to do with living things and the natural world around them

endangered *(in-DAYN-juhrd)* when a type of plant or animal is at risk of dying out

equinoxes *(EK-win-ox-ez)* the times of year when there are equal lengths of day and night, usually March 21 and September 23

habitat *(HAB-uh-tat)* the natural place where a plant or animal lives

monarchy *(MON-ahr-kee)* a type of government that is ruled by one person, such as a king or queen

natural resources *(NACH-ur-uhl REE-sohr-siz)* materials found in nature, such as oil, trees, and minerals, that are used by humans

pilgrimage *(PIL-gruh-mij)* a long journey taken for religious reasons, usually to a holy place

urban *(UR-bin)* having to do with cities

Victorian *(vik-TOR-ee-in)* from the time of Queen Victoria, who ruled over Great Britain from 1837 to 1901

FOR MORE INFORMATION

BOOKS

Hubbard, Ben. *Samurai Warriors.* New York: Cavendish Square Publishing, 2017.

Kelly, Tracy. *The Culture and Recipes of Japan.* Buffalo: PowerKids Press, 2017.

Nobleman, Marc Tyler. *Thirty Minutes over Oregon: A Story from World War II.* Boston: Houghton Mifflin Harcourt, 2018.

WEB SITES

DCG Worldwide Inc.—All About Sushi Guide
https://www.allaboutsushiguide.com
Expand your knowledge of sushi, including history, dining etiquette, recipes, and more.

Digital Dialects—Japanese Language Games
http://www.digitaldialects.com/Japanese.htm
Learn and practice Japanese words and phrases with these interactive games.

National Geographic Kids—Japan
https://kids.nationalgeographic.com/explore/countries/japan
Read more about the history, government, and culture of Japan.

INDEX

ABOUT THE AUTHOR

Leah Kaminski loves international travel. She especially likes learning about the culture and ecology of other countries. Leah lives with her husband and baby boy in Chicago, where she teaches, writes poetry, and writes books like this one.